D1258155

NOVEMBER TWENTY SIX NINETEEN HUNDRED SIXTY THREE

Poem by Wendell Berry

Drawings by Ben Shahn

GEORGE BRAZILLER NEW YORK

NOVEMBER
TWENTY SIX
NINETEEN
HUNDRED
SIXTY THREE

 For information address the publisher, George Braziller, Inc., 215 Park Avenue South, New York 3 *Library of Congress Catalog Number: 64-19345*

FIRST EDITION PRINTED IN THE UNITED STATES OF AMERICA

Each one of us wanted to cry out, somehow to express our shock and horror at the assassination of the President. Each one of us tried to say in conversation what we felt, but essentially we were mute. Our gestures were helpless; our impulses somehow to monumentalize those days, to hold them and not let them sink into banality and acceptance — such impulses were doomed to failure, to that very acceptance which we wanted to avoid.

It was shortly after those shattering few days that the following poem appeared in *The Nation*. I found it extraordinarily moving. It was right in every way; it was modest and unrhetorical. It examined soberly and sensitively just this event in its every detail. Its images were the images of those days, no others. In so sharply scrutinizing his own feelings, the poet has discovered with an uncanny exactness all our feelings. His words have created a certain monument, not pretentious, but real, and shared.

When I read the poem, I wanted it preserved, read, not lost in the pages of a last week's magazine. I turned it into a book, accompanied by the images that it invokes for me. I have hoped, in some small way, to help monumentalize those days so that we may not so soon become inured to an unacceptable violence, a failure, a profound sadness.

Ben Shahn

WE KNOW
THE WINTER EARTH
UPON THE BODY
OF THE YOUNG
PRESIDENT,
AND THE EARLY DARK
FALLING;

WE KNOW
THE VEINS
GROWN QUIET
IN HIS TEMPLES AND
WRISTS, AND HIS HANDS
AND EYES
GROWN QUIET;

WE KNOW
HIS NAME WRITTEN
IN THE BLACK CAPITALS
OF HIS DEATH,
AND THE MOURNERS
STANDING IN THE RAIN,
AND THE LEAVES
FALLING;

WE KNOW
HIS DEATH'S HORSES
AND DRUMS;
THE ROSES, BELLS,
CANDLES, CROSSES;
THE FACES
HIDDEN IN VEILS;

WE KNOW
THE CHILDREN
WHO BEGIN
THE YOUTH OF LOSS
GREATER THAN
THEY CAN DREAM
NOW;

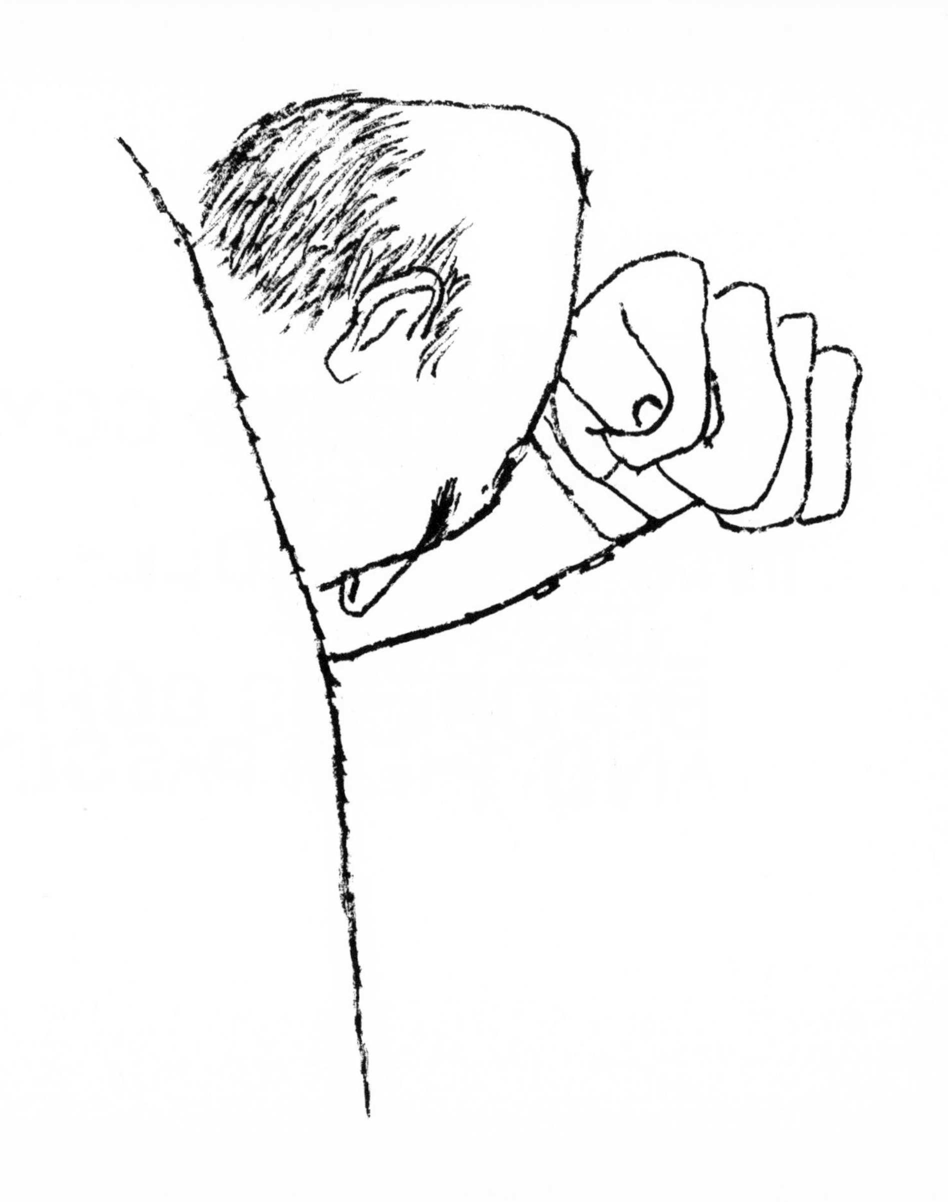

WE KNOW
THE NIGHTLONG COMING
OF FACES
INTO THE CANDLE-
LIGHT
BEFORE HIS COFFIN,
AND THEIR PASSING;

WE KNOW
THE MOUTH OF THE GRAVE
WAITING,
THE BUGLE AND RIFLES,
    THE MOURNERS
    TURNING
    AWAY;

WE KNOW
THE YOUNG DEAD BODY
CARRIED
IN THE EARTH
INTO THE FIRST
DEEP NIGHT
OF ITS ABSENCE;

HERE
EVERY
THERE
WHERE
3
29
14
DR UGS
UNCH

WE KNOW
OUR STREETS AND DAYS
SLOWLY OPENING
INTO THE TIME
    HE IS NOT ALIVE,
    FILLING WITH
    OUR FOOTSTEPS
    AND VOICES;

WE KNOW
OURSELVES,
THE BEARERS
OF THE LIGHT
OF THE EARTH
HE IS GIVEN TO,
AND OF THE LIGHT OF
ALL HIS LOST DAYS;

WE KNOW
THE LONG APPROACH
OF SUMMERS TOWARD THE
HEALED GROUND
WHERE HE WILL BE
WAITING,
NO LONGER THE KEEPER
OF WHAT HE WAS.

This book was lettered and illustrated by Ben Shahn
Printed at The Meriden Gravure Company, Meriden, Connecticut,
on Linweave Early American paper
Bound by Haddon Craftsmen, Inc., Scranton, Pennsylvania

The poem *November 26, 1963* originally appeared in *The Nation*
and is reprinted with the permission of the editors of that magazine.